T0273553

On Self-Hatred

Other books in this series:
Why You Will Marry the Wrong Person
On Confidence
How to Find Love
Why We Hate Cheap Things
Self-Knowledge
The Sorrows of Work
The Sorrows of Love
What Is Culture For?
What is Psychotherapy?
How to Reform Capitalism

On Self-Hatred

The School of Life

Published in 2022 by The School of Life
First published in the USA in 2023
930 High Road, London, N12 9RT
Copyright © The School of Life 2022
Designed by Marcia Mihotich
Typeset by Kerrypress
Printed in Lithuania by Balto Print

A proportion of this book has appeared online at
www.theschooloflife.com/articles

Every effort has been made to contact the copyright holders of the
material reproduced in this book. If any have been inadvertently
overlooked, the publisher will be pleased to make restitution at
the earliest opportunity.

The School of Life publishes a range of books on essential topics
in psychological and emotional life, including relationships,
parenting, friendship, careers and fulfilment. The aim is always
to help us to understand ourselves better – and thereby to grow
calmer, less confused and more purposeful. Discover our full
range of titles, including books for children, here:
www.theschooloflife.com/books

The School of Life also offers a comprehensive therapy service,
which complements, and draws upon, our published works:
www.theschooloflife.com/therapy.

www.theschooloflife.com

ISBN 978-1-912891-87-0

10 9 8 7 6 5 4 3

Contents

I

Introduction
Page 7

II

Audit
Page 15

III

The Consequences of Self-Hatred
Page 21

IV

The Origins of Self-Hatred
Page 61

V

The Art of Self-Acceptance
Page 89

VI

Towards a More Self-Accepting Life
Page 131

I
Introduction

Behind a lot of mental illness is an ingredient that we're not used to considering on its own as an agent of our unhappiness: self-hatred. We may feel as if we are just worried about the future, unable to overcome regrets or uncomfortable around other people, but first and foremost we may be experts at hating ourselves. Self-hatred deserves to be recognised and studied as one of the greatest causes of our misery, responsible for more despair, loneliness and suicides than almost any other affliction of our troublesome minds.

Self-hatred is the bitter fruit of an ingrained sense of what we *should* be like. We hate the way we are because, somewhere in our evolution, we picked up some unyielding ideas about the way we *should* be: what we *should* have achieved, how many mistakes we *should* have made, how we *should* look, what others *should* be saying about us. We carry within us a gamut of expectations that remorselessly torment us and inflict on us some of the many symptoms of self-hatred: a tense spine, insomnia, malfunctioning bowels, a longing for but also discomfort about our achievements, a feeling of dread and, in the wake of crises, a desire to kill ourselves.

One of the reasons why self-hatred can be so hard to

overcome is the belief that its opposite and cure lies with something called *self-love*, a belief that we will finally cease to hate ourselves when we learn to admire, delight in and cherish our own being. It sounds logical and kindly enough, and we are frequently nudged to do this: we are invited to look at ourselves in the mirror afresh and see the beauty in our features; we are encouraged to celebrate our strengths and our innate resourcefulness, creativity and power.

There is kindness in such advice, but the results can be paradoxical. Unable to locate the wonder that we are being drawn to contemplate, we may be submerged beneath a new and yet more vicious wave of self-hatred; we need to add a failure at self-love to our list of defeats. Or else, seduced into over-eager admiration, we may lose contact with important sources of self-scepticism and modesty.

The cure for self-hatred does not lie in heightening self-love, but in fostering self-acceptance. Self-acceptance does not require us to overcome every vestige of self-criticism. It is compatible with a realistic appraisal of our strengths and weaknesses. While practising self-acceptance, we can remain in many ways sorrowful about, and suspicious of, ourselves.

The cure for self-hatred does not lie in heightening self-love, but in fostering self-acceptance.

A self-hating person not only dislikes themselves, they cannot get over their dislike; they remain tied to their hatred by the shortest of nooses. Every new day, they must return to self-recrimination: they cannot forget all the daft moves they made; they refuse to tolerate their appearance; they can't let go of the idea of where they should be in their careers by now; they never forget the mean things others are saying.

Behind this repetitiveness lies not only masochism, but a manic attachment to the possibility of a perfect life. Perfectionism turns out to be a secret fuel for self-hatred. However modest the self-hating person might outwardly seem, inside they are in agony because they refuse to surrender their attachment to being potentially flawless, physically beautiful, morally pure, error-free and wholly successful in the eyes of the world.

Self-acceptance points in another direction: it starts with the certainty that to be human is to err, to fail, to be foolish, to have ugly sides, to make mistakes, to age, to die and, along the way, never to be far from ridiculousness, fatuousness and idiocy. These are not criticisms of any one person or matters for individual reproof; they are facts about the human race. The self-accepting person can take these bitter ideas on board with grace and a healthy measure of humour – the most sophisticated response to the gap between our expectations and our reality. The self-accepting are not surprised by evidence of where they have fallen short; they navigate the world with a strong sense of their inherent ridiculousness.

Ultimately we have to measure the worth of negative emotions by their power to keep us alive. By this standard, there is surely an occasional role for self-dissatisfaction and guilt, for regret and melancholy. But what serves no purpose is a long-term determined hatred of one's own being.

We are all a bit awful – it is a fact of being human – yet however much this may have grimly fascinated and detained us until now, we should gradually let go of this idea in order to fulfil our true purpose on the earth, which is to be of maximal use to other people, in whatever way we can, in the time we have left. Self-hatred may have underpinned the past; it does not need to be our future.

II
Audit

One of the odder features of self-hatred is that it may escape our notice for the greater part of our lives. We may not be aware that we don't like ourselves very much, even as the sickness of self-hatred wreaks havoc across a range of psychological situations and opportunities.

Our self-suspicion tends to linger in undiagnosed forms. We miss the extent to which we can suffer from endemic self-loathing and how a once acceptable and perhaps invigorating form of self-questioning has turned into a lacerating sequence of attacks on everything we are and do. Paradoxically, we may be both depressed about ourselves and oblivious that we are.

In order to know what we are up against, we should take a measure of our sense of self. For this, we might resort to that simple but helpful psychological tool, the questionnaire. We can ask to what extent we might agree with the following sentences on a scale of one to ten, ten meaning very much, one indicating not at all.

- *If people knew who I really was, they would be horrified.*
- *The inside of me is appalling.*
- *Often, I can't bear who I am.*
- *I'm disgusting.*

- *I'm shameful.*
- *I'm weak.*
- *Others have a good cause to hate and harm me.*
- *It's only a matter of time before terrible things happen to me, given who I am.*
- *I'm sexually revolting.*
- *I am physically repulsive.*
- *I am unworthy of being forgiven.*
- *I am a fitting target for ridicule.*
- *I am bound to fail.*
- *I don't deserve much sympathy.*
- *People often see me in the street and feel contempt.*
- *I have acted badly across my whole life.*
- *There is something fundamentally wrong with me.*

We don't need to do careful sums to arrive at an indicative picture at speed. Some of us will be reaching for tens on pretty much every occasion; others will be puzzled by the whole exercise. This book is not for them.

If we find ourselves reaching for high numbers, we may be tempted to come to a powerful yet mistaken conclusion: that we are terrible people. The reality is at once less personally damning and far more redemptive: we aren't so terrible at all; we are just very ill. The questionnaire is telling us about an affliction, not about our past or what we deserve or who we really are. The very extremity of our answers should signal that something is afoot that far exceeds what any human is ever owed. We aren't intolerably wicked; we are in the grip of a cruel sickness that systematically destroys any confidence or generosity we might feel towards ourselves. We are treating ourselves with a violence and pitilessness we wouldn't think of bestowing upon our worst enemies. We have, somehow, ended up considering the person we have to accompany through life with an unparalleled degree of coldness and disdain.

It is time to come to terms with our suffering, and to refuse the delusion and meanness of self-hatred.

III

The Consequences
of Self-Hatred

Identifying the weed

If self-hatred is an illness that doesn't present itself clearly for diagnosis, we must sharpen our awareness of its varied and crafty manifestations, so that we can more quickly identify, interrogate and challenge it.

We need to be able to see that beneath many varied phenomena, the same essential dynamic is at play. It might look as if we are dealing with a variety of issues – self-sabotage, paranoia, grandiosity or suicidal thoughts – but what is unfolding below the surface is often exactly the same disease: an asphyxiating dislike of ourselves.

We should learn to spot the poisonous weed of self-hatred in a variety of settings and to be appropriately impressed by its inventiveness and its tenacity; it can wend its way around the trunks of the proudest trees and rob the healthiest plants of their nutrients.

What follows is a journey through some of the sicknesses of the soul with which we should want finally to grow impatient and uncowed.

High achievement

At first glance, it might seem as though the people we term high achievers could not possibly have any problem with self-hatred: they are the ones who did exceptionally well in exams, whom the teachers admired, who won places at the best universities, who graduated with honours, who got into law and medical schools, who founded thriving businesses, who live in the wealthiest parts of town, who are up early in the morning preparing themselves healthy breakfasts before a day of important meetings. Surely we can't impute that these people might be suffering from the ravages of self-disgust? Except, of course, that it would rarely occur to anyone who did not harbour a high degree of self-suspicion to undertake so many outsize efforts to impress and to make a mark upon the world.

Many high achievers, for all their accomplishments, cannot trust in a basic idea: that it might be acceptable to be themselves, outside of any acclaim, notice or distinction. Simply being is not enough; their right to exist can only be assured by constant *doing*. Their frantic activity masks an underlying unquenchable doubt as to their acceptability. Holidays are a particular trial; free time has been carefully expunged from their diaries, and it may have been many years since they enjoyed a day without commitments. The moment that they are at a loose end, anxiety arises: What are they meant to be doing? What have they forgotten to take care of?

No one can doubt what we owe to the high achievers. They are the ones who build the skyscrapers, who examine distant planets, who drive the stock market to new heights, who start businesses and write films and books. We would be all the poorer without them.

But our respect shouldn't rob us of our ability to appraise the costs that their ways of life exact. The wealth of nations is built upon the troubles of the individual psyche. The high achievers have been driven to act not simply from talent or creativity, energy and skill (though these are no doubt present as well) but from a primordial sense that there is something shameful about them in their basic state, and that they must hence clothe themselves in the garments of success to escape the humiliation of their true selves.

No wonder that their efforts are so often self-defeating. It may seem as if they were after money, power, acclaim and distinction, but these are merely substitutes for their fundamental but unknown goal: a sense of basic adequacy. The disjuncture explains the curious lassitude and sadness that may accompany high achievers at some of their moments of greatest triumph. Finally, they have sold the company. At last they have won an international prize. But they are likely to feel hollow in the days and years that follow, as they confusedly recognise that every possible achievement has been gained but that none of it has been sufficient to quell the pain and restlessness within.

It can be counted as close to good fortune if high achievers stumble and fail somewhere along their journey, if they are tripped up by an unexpected bankruptcy, scandal or economic downturn. The reversal may prompt a mental breakdown and a period of rest. In this there is a sliver of hope, for it contains a chance to see that their manic pursuit of success was masking a terror about unloveability, which now has a chance to be quelled in more realistic and effective ways. There is an opportunity to acknowledge that one has been playing the wrong game all along, and that the true problem never had anything to do with a lack of prizes, and everything to do with a burning conviction that one might need so many of them.

It is a measure of our collective delusion that we are so ready to be proud of high achievers and so slow to detect the wound that powers them on. It would be a less gilded world, but also a far happier one, in which we were readier to reassure the self-hating titans of success that they were worthy of love all along.

Romantic masochism

There is a particular kind of romantic pilgrim whose love life attracts a high degree of sympathy. Despite their best intentions and apparently ceaseless efforts, they seem fated to move from one unsatisfying candidate to another without ever being able to settle. One lover turned out to be secretly married to someone else; another, after an initial period of enthusiasm, never called back and a third turned out to be an alcoholic and violent. We can only express sympathy for what seems like a run of exceptional bad luck.

Yet if one examines the problem at closer range, we're liable to find that bad luck can only explain so much, and that there has been a process of careful curation at work too. The unfortunate lover has not simply stumbled upon a succession of frustrating or mean-minded partners;

they have actively sought these out and invited them in while simultaneously ensuring that no kinder candidate could ever gain a foothold. They still deserve sympathy, but not for the problem they have ostensibly complained about.

It is logical to imagine that what we want in love is someone who will treat us with respect and tenderness, loyalty and thoughtfulness. But however much these may sound desirable in theory, in reality, such qualities are liable to provoke in some huge anxieties and, on occasion, revulsion.

It might seem uncomplicatedly beautiful if someone makes us breakfast in bed, gives us endearing nicknames, tells us how much they miss us, cries a little when we go away on a long trip and thoughtfully offers us a teddy bear to pack in our case. There could surely be nothing nicer – except, that is, if we are in doubt as to our own value.

For the self-hating ones among us, such attentions are likely to trigger acute discomfort and anxiety: Why does our lover seem to think so much better of us than we think of ourselves? Why do they hold us in such high esteem when we cannot bear our own reflection? How have we come to be so heroic in their eyes when we are so despicable in our own? Why do they call us beautiful and kind, intelligent and thoughtful when we feel as if we are none of these things? Their attentions end up having to be met with all the disdain we accord to false flatterers. We are sickened to receive gifts that we are sure we do not deserve.

It's as an escape from this form of nausea that we may run into the arms of people who can be relied upon to be cruel to us. They aren't delighted when we walk into a room; they have no interest in our childhoods or what happened to us today; they show no particular enthusiasm for sleeping with us; they flirt with others and give us no guarantee that the relationship will survive until tomorrow. It sounds appalling, and in a sense it is, but it may feel a lot less appalling than to be showered by a kindness we are certain that we have never earnt. At least the meanness on display accords with our assessment of ourselves.

Whatever we may claim, there are almost always a host of potential romantic partners ready to treat us nicely; it is just that, with no awareness of the process, we have probably become experts at dismissing them, tossing them aside with terms like 'boring' or 'uninspiring'. By this we really mean: uninclined to think as badly of us as we think of ourselves, or unlikely to make us suffer in the way we need to suffer in order to feel we are receiving the sort of attention that befits us.

In truth, these kind people are generally very far from dull or stupid. They have spotted something about us that we have not yet taken on board: that we are not appalling and that, beneath our defences, we remain kind, sweet and worthy. These observers just frighten us because, with their kindness, they challenge a fundamental pillar of our psychology: the idea that we are owed punishment. We will learn to see many such kind lovers waiting for us in the wings, and will be far readier to let them into our affections the moment we can accept that, for all our many (yet utterly normal) flaws, we don't deserve to be humiliated and frustrated for the rest of our lives.

Looks

When we are very concerned about certain of our physical features – the nose that is too large, the eyes that are slightly too far apart, the hair that is not as lustrous as it should be – we miss an overall point about our relationship to our appearance: how beautiful we feel has nothing to do with the objective structure of our face or body; our self-assessments are based on our relative degrees of self-love and self-contempt.

There are people of ideal proportions and exceptional lustre who cannot bear what they see in the mirror, and others who can contemplate a less than svelte stomach or a no longer so supple kind of skin with indifference and defiant good humour. At a tragic extreme, there are heart-breakingly fine-looking people who starve themselves to ill health and eventually death out of a certainty, immune to every logical argument, of their own unsightliness.

We are surrounded by industries that seek to help us to improve how we look: dieticians who are on hand to reduce our waistlines; aerobic teachers who offer to tone us; beauticians who will equip us with foundation and mascara. But however well-meaning their efforts, they fail to grasp the sources of a healthy regard for one's own appearance.

The issue is not whether we look extraordinary today, but whether or not we were, once upon a time, when we were small and defenceless before the judgements of those who cared for us, sufficiently loved for our essence. This will decide whether the vagaries of our appearance can later on be a subject of negligible concern to us – or not. The truly blessed among us are not those with perfect symmetry; they are those whose past affords them the luxury not to care too much what the mirror happens to say.

The way to help someone feel beautiful is not to compliment them on their looks, it is to take an interest in and delight in their psychological essence. When we meet those who worry that they are not attractive enough, we should not rush in with physical compliments; this is only to foster and unwittingly reward an aggravating criterion of judgement. We should learn to spot the wound in their early relationships that has made it so hard for them to trust that they could matter to others in their basic state and that therefore perpetually evokes in them an unflattering self-image.

They are not 'ugly' per se; they were, when it mattered, left painfully unloved and ignored to an extent that they are liable never to have recognised or mourned adequately. Their arrival in the world did not delight a few people as it should have done, and they therefore need compassion, sympathy and emotional validation far more than they will require the tools of outward beautification. Feeling ugly stems from a deficit of love, not of beauty.

Shyness

A lack of confidence is often put down to something we call shyness. But beneath shyness, there may lie something more surprising, pernicious and poignant. We suffer from a suspicion of ourselves that gives us a sense that other people will always have good reasons to dislike us, to think ill of us, to question our motives and to mock us. We then become scared of the world, speak in a small voice, don't dare to show our face at gatherings and are frightened of social occasions because we fear that we are ideal targets for ridicule and disdain. Our shy manner is the pre-emptive stance we adopt in the face of the blows we feel that other people want to land on us. Our shyness is rooted in a sense of unworthiness.

As shy people, when we find ourselves in a foreign city in which we know no one, we can be thrown into panic at the prospect of having to enter a busy restaurant and order a meal on our own. Dogged by a feeling that no one especially wants to know us, that we are outside the charmed circle of the popular and the desirable, we are sure that our repulsiveness will be noticed by others and that we will be the target of sneering and viciousness. We unknowingly impute to strangers the nasty comments that we are experts at making to ourselves; our self-image returns to haunt us in the assumed views of others. We imagine that groups of friends will take mean delight in our solitary state and read into it appalling conclusions about our nature. They will see right through our veneer of competence and adulthood and detect the deformed and unfinished creature we have felt like since the start. They will know how desperate we have been to win friends and how pitiful and isolated we are. Even the waiter will fight to restrain their desire to giggle at our expense in the kitchen.

A comparable fear haunts us at the idea of going into a clothes shop. The sales attendant will surely immediately sense how unfit we are to lay claim to the stylishness on offer. They may suspect we lack the money; they will be appalled by our physique. We lack the right to pamper our own bodies.

It can be as much of a hurdle to attend a party. Here too our fundamental imagined awfulness is perpetually at risk of being noticed and exploited by others. As we try to join a group of people chatting animatedly, we dread that they will swiftly realise how unfunny we are, how craven our nature is and how peculiar and damned we are at our core.

The novelist Franz Kafka, who hated himself with rare energy, famously imagined himself into the role of a cockroach. This move of the imagination will feel familiar to anyone sick with self-disdain. We, the self-hating ones, spontaneously identify with all the stranger, less photogenic animals: rhinoceroses, blobfish, spiders, warthogs, elephant seals ... We skulk in corners, we run away from our shadow, we live in fear of being swatted away and killed.

It is no surprise if, against such an internal background, we end up 'shy'. The solution is not to urge us blithely to be more confident. It is to help us to take stock of our feelings about ourselves that we have ascribed to an audience that is in reality far more innocent and unconcerned than we ever imagine. We need to trace our self-hatred back to its origins, repatriate and localise it and drain it of its power to infect our views of those we encounter. Everyone else isn't jeering, or bored or convinced of our revoltingness;

these are our certainties, not theirs. We don't have to whisper in a circumspect manner and enter each new conversation, restaurant or shop with a sheepish air of apology. We can cast aside our introverted circumspection once we realise the distortions of our self-perception, and can come to believe in a world that has far better things to do than to despise us.

Impostor syndrome

There is a peculiar affliction that may befall those who have spent many patient years working at their professional goals and are finally within striking distance of mastery and success. Just as they are called upon to take the next step in their progress – managing a team, making speeches, putting on their uniform – they are thrown into a state of paralysis and terror that threatens to undermine their hard-won opportunities. They may have to run away from the podium or meeting room; they may break into a sweat or develop a speech impediment or a debilitating stomach complaint. They turn into scared children immobilised by the challenges of an adult role.

What the sufferer of the so-called impostor syndrome cannot get over is a sense of how much in their own character renders them unfit for the dignity and responsibility of higher office. They cannot forget the extent of their ignorance, the scale of their self-doubt, and their ongoing degrees of idiocy, apprehension and foolishness. They scan the faces and biographies of those they seek to emulate and see in them no evidence of anything akin to their own weaknesses. No one else in their new rank seems as scared, doubtful, immature or weak as they know themselves to be. No one else has such silly daydreams or harbours as much laziness and cowardice. Their scrupulous awareness of their deficiencies acts as a definitive argument against their own advancement.

In reality, sufferers of impostor syndrome are not any more unsuited to responsibility than anyone else; they simply hate themselves with greater relentlessness. They are unable to get the right perspective on their flaws and cannot set these within a broad and sympathetic understanding of our species' inherent imperfections. They aren't guilty of more mistakes; they have a more tyrannous and narrowly focused conscience. A degree of absurdity that they share with every other human has been allowed to grow into a conclusive argument against the possibility of a successful life.

At base, sufferers of the syndrome don't know other people well enough. Whether through subterfuge or happenstance, they have been denied a liberating acquaintance with the recesses of the minds of those around them. They haven't taken on board that almost every piece of madness, deviousness or miscalculation that exists in their heads will have a corollary in those of others. They have believed in the self-advertisements of others.

Somewhere during their early development, these sufferers were likely to have been held to a far higher account than other children. They were denied an experience of loving forgiveness for all the stumbling steps that naturally belong to our development. Ordinary mistakes and anxieties attracted undue censure and shame, as if they were uniquely wicked for being wholly normal. The result is that these sufferers now shout at and attack themselves without reprieve when health would mandate clemency and absolution.

If one is offering reassurance to those suffering from impostor syndrome, we should beware of emphasising how many strengths and qualities they actually possess. We should instead, with greater kindness and effectiveness, accept the record of their doubts and frailties but then allow them to see how normal and unalarming these are. They aren't evidence that the sufferers are fated to be forever 'children' who can't cope; there are just no true 'adults' anywhere, in the sense of paragons of fearlessness and virtue. There are lots of grown-up people who are more or less holding it together in the face of their own psychological eccentricities, putting on a good show most of the time, doing their best and occasionally running home to sob and despair, panic and scream. No one is ever as competent as they feel they should be; what varies is how tolerant people can be of their own incompetence.

Those anxious about their success are not impostors; they have all the same attributes as anyone else who has ever managed to forge a satisfying career. The whole of sensible professional life is in many ways a glorified act, a beautiful, concealed charade, that we should feel no compunction about joining and thriving in. Our preposterous aspects should never be an argument for shame or against success.

People pleasing

There is a kind of person who seems, on initial acquaintance, to be astonishingly in agreement with us on all major and minor topics. Whatever political statement we make wins their accord. Wherever we want to go chimes with their wishes. They have come to identical conclusions on every book and film we mention. They find exactly the same things funny; they were just about to suggest exactly the same kind of sandwich filling for lunch.

It seems as if we have chanced upon a long-lost twin or divine soulmate, but the reality is more prosaic and complicated. The other's boundless propensity to be aligned with us springs not from some magical twinship of the psyche, but from their terror of the consequences of disagreement. The people pleaser has imbibed an impression that voicing contrary opinions, from what to eat to how to run a company or a nation, will be met with titanic fury or vengeful disappointment. They agree with us from a sense that it would be impossible to say authentically what they thought and survive as an object of regard and affection.

The people pleaser is likely to have started life as the offspring of a parent with particular ruthlessness around diverging views. In the initial family setting, there might have been only one right way to organise a meal, one right place to go on holiday and one right way to polish shoes, and it was certainly not for a child to decide which these might be. Alternatively, a beloved but fragile-seeming parent might have collapsed at the slightest sign of protest or independence, and implicitly accused a child of endangering their sanity or life through their 'wilfulness'.

As a result, the people pleaser labours under a punishing internal directive never to utter their own thoughts. Or, worse, they may have stopped even having them; they aren't just keeping quiet, they have nothing left to keep quiet about. They still have ringing in their ears, perhaps many decades after they first heard them, voices that advise them in the sternest ways not to be so silly, to shut up and listen, to not get above their station and to obey their betters. Self-hatred has destroyed the development of their own minds.

Liberation begins with an idea that might at first sound disorienting and frightening: that whatever the people pleaser's early experience might have taught them, most humans do not in fact find those who agree with them on everything very pleasing. Despite the occasional charms of compliance, an unbounded servility grates, and for good reason: we sense the danger in such passivity, we know that someone who will tell us only what we want to hear will be a risk to our understanding of the world and keep us blind to vital sources of challenging information. Paradoxically, people pleasing doesn't please.

Along the way, these unfortunates must be given a chance to trust in an idea that would at one time have seemed deeply taboo: that they can afford to think of themselves as centres of original perception and novel thoughts, some of which may be of supreme importance and validity, even when they don't immediately align with fashionable opinion or received wisdom.

Through the case of people pleasers, we glimpse the surprising origins of good thinking in the experience of love. Feeling loved is what enables us to use our minds imaginatively and freely. To have felt truly cared for is to have surmised that we do not need to toe the line faithfully at all points in our speculations and that others can cherish us even as we raise contrasting or challenging points of view. What the lucky ones among us understood from the outset, people pleasers must learn painfully and intellectually: that with sufficient self-love, it need not always feel like an impossible gamble to nurture and disclose the contents of our own minds.

Anxiety

One of the greatest of mental afflictions is anxiety, by which we mean not the odd worry about this or that, but a constant, dawn-till-dusk feeling of apprehension and dread, either about one repetitively large and torturous thing, or a seemingly random and ever-expanding medley of smaller concerns. As sufferers of chronic anxiety, phenomena that more robust people take in their stride have the power to derail and shutter our minds: we worry intensely about what others are thinking, about what gossip might be spread about us, about how our enemies might bring us down, about the risks of being sacked and mocked, about the possibilities of being attacked, made homeless or sent to prison.

A standard contemporary response is to take pills to dampen our overactive imaginations. We end up mildly sedated, but at least we have a few hours of respite from our infernal inner broadcasts of catastrophic foreboding.

Yet adjusting our mental chemistry isn't an alternative to wondering why we have ended up so afraid in the first place. We worry an uncommon amount not because we are more at risk than anyone else but, arguably, because we dislike ourselves more intensely; the root of anxiety lies in the psychological cancer of self-hatred. The first question to investigate with a very anxious person is therefore not what they are so worried about but how they came to be so unfriendly to themselves.

If we are the wretches that we at some level suspect we might be, then it is only natural to suspect that we must be due a comeuppance: bad things must eventually befall the so-called bad people we are certain we are. Any mildly positive or optimistic event has to be questioned and denigrated because it runs contrary to our latent impression of ourselves. It simply doesn't feel possible or natural that everything could be okay, given how much at heart we don't think we are okay.

The route to calm requires that we start in an odd-sounding place: with our estimation of ourselves. So long as we continue to be suspicious of who we are, the world will seem like a very dangerous place. It must surely be only a matter of time until the mockery and humiliation begin. But if we can find enough room to question and chip away at our self-dislike, then we may have the opportunity to put a little distance between our rational minds and our fears.

When we feel panic descending, we should have the confidence to ignore our ostensible targets of concern. We may not need to check for the hundredth time that we haven't said anything wrong or offended someone. We can change the subject in our consciousness and grow curious as to why one part of us should feel so inclined to torment and worry the other. We may not be living in such a scary universe; we may just have grown up to be highly opposed to ourselves, an original wound that, from now on, deserves to be the true object of our vigilance and concern.

Perfectionism

There is a kind of person who seems at first glance to have an admirable degree of self-motivation, thoroughness and drive. They are up at dawn, they rarely take holidays, they are always sneaking in an extra hour or two of work. Their bosses are highly impressed, they are constantly promoted, their grades have been excellent since primary school, they never miss an appointment or turn in a piece of work that is less than stellar.

We like to say that such a person has high standards; we might even anoint them with the term 'perfectionist'. It might seem churlish to locate any problems here. Why complain about a somewhat overzealous devotion to perfection in a troubled and lackadaisical world? There could surely be nothing too awful about high exactitude? What could be so imperfect about perfectionism?

The concern is not so much with the work of the perfectionist (its recipients are in a privileged position) as with the state of their soul. Perfectionism does not spring primarily from a love of perfection in and of itself. It has its origins in the far more regrettable feeling of never being good enough. It is rooted in self-hatred, sparked by memories of being disapproved of or neglected by those who should have esteemed us warmly in childhood.

We become perfectionists from a primary sense of being unworthy, uninteresting, flawed, a disappointment, a let-down, a nuisance. So powerful is this sense, so appalling is its pressure on our psyches, we are prepared to do more or less anything to expunge it. Working all hours, currying favour with authority, doing twice as much as the next person – these are the tools with which we seek to cleanse our apparently undeserving selves.

One part of the mind promises the other that the completion of the next challenge will finally usher in peace. We can be good at pretending that our ambitions are sane, but our work has a Sisyphean dimension: no sooner have we rolled our working boulder up the hill than it will tumble back down again. There will never be a point of rest or a lasting feeling of completion. In truth, we are ill rather than driven.

We aren't interested in perfect work at all: we are trying to escape from a feeling of being awful people, and work simply happens to be the medium through which we strive to grow tolerable in our own eyes. But because our problem didn't begin with work, work can never prove the solution.

Our real goal is not, as we think, to be an ideal employee or professional, it is to feel acceptable. But responsibility for a sense of acceptance cannot be handed over to our bosses or customers or a ceaselessly demanding capitalist system; these will never let us rest easy because it is in their nature, with no evil intent, always to demand more.

We need to shift our sense of where our drive is coming from. We are not unnaturally interested in working perfectly, we are labouring under an unusually intense impression that we are dreadful people – a problem for which working harder cannot be the answer.

We need to allow ourselves to imagine that we deserved to be accepted from the start and that it cannot forever be our fault in our minds that we were not. It is not up to us to try to prove that we have a right to exist. It is asking too much of ourselves to have to experience a referendum on our legitimacy every time we hand in a report, every exam we have to pass, every customer we have to serve.

Working well is an admirable goal, but it becomes a symptom of mental perturbation when it becomes the cover for a secret aspiration to correct a deficit of early love. We should welcome an ability to tolerate periods of laziness, not because we are congenitally idle, but because it is a sign that we have learnt to speak more kindly to ourselves and to be appropriately angry with those who could not at the outset accept us for who we were without a surfeit of trophies and prizes.

Grandiosity

In looking to understand self-hatred, we should consider a subsection of people who seem pleased with everything they are and do. They radiate self-contentment and pride, even if it isn't always apparent on what their extreme satisfaction with themselves rests. They dominate conversations, they walk with their heads held high, they let everyone know that they have arrived in the building. They aren't great listeners, of course; your stories and dilemmas understandably have to be relegated when there is so much that is glorious and intriguing about their own lives.

If ever they suffer a shortfall in respect (for example, in a restaurant or in a shop), they don't hesitate to correct the problem; they furiously bang the airline business class check-in desk or ask the terrified waiter – who may have brought them the wrong kind of mustard – if they know with whom they are dealing. Those of meeker temperament can only look on with a mixture of envy, admiration and a touch of horror and wonder how such characters could have come to harbour such relentless faith in themselves.

The answer is not what we might expect. However much self-hatred may be responsible for low self-confidence, even greater amounts of self-hatred tend to be at play in the pattern of behaviour we term grandiosity. A person needs to hate themselves to a truly uncommon degree in order to insist that everyone must listen to what they have to say, that no one can disagree and that they are always the most important person in the room. Outsized regard for oneself is not the outcome of boundless self-love, it is the diseased flower of a terrified, self-doubting mind.

In the childhood of the grandiose person, one can expect to find a confusion of emotional ingredients: these unfortunates may have been built up to immense heights by a parent who was both seemingly on their side and yet unpredictable and distracted in their attentions. The parent may have told the child that they were exceptionally gifted and destined for glory, but then done nothing to help them to know why and how this might be the case. They might have abandoned the family home or spent a lot of time depressed or more interested in other people. The ostensible message was that the child was a prodigy – but why in that case did the parent never bother to listen to them properly, to sympathise with their reality and to be patient with their growing pains? The child was left to inhabit a golden role that they never really understood why they had been accorded or knew how to live up to.

The grandiose person now insists on their specialness with such ferocity because they are inwardly close to a terrifying prospect: that they may just be average, that they were actually unloved early on, that they were at one time bigged up yet also fundamentally alone and uncared for. A healthy relationship to ourselves requires that we gracefully take on board certain challenging realities: that we may have said something wrong, that we aren't as good as we had hoped, that we still need to learn a lot. With sufficient self-love, we can absorb such blows without collapse. We have enough inner warmth to bear the sharp winds of scepticism. We like ourselves enough that we don't always need to be right; we are happy enough with who we are not to have to insist on our specialness.

No such luxury is afforded to the grandiose. One millimetre away from the baroque scaffolding of their self-confidence lies a devastating and raw landscape of utter nullity. No one has ever been kind enough to let them fail and still be cared for, to let them say stupid things and still be cherished. It is no wonder that they speak so loudly and cannot risk the merest moment of humiliation. It requires a lot of self-love to accept that one may be a bit of a fool of whom most people don't think very much and who will die leaving the universe undisturbed. It is a sign of immense psychological privilege to know how to be ordinary.

What is sad about the grandiose is that their illness renders other people unlikely to step forward to offer them the kindness they need. The last thing that the over-confident appear to require is reassurance. It takes an advanced level of imagination to determine that beneath the shouting, incensed, puce-faced customer there may lie a frightened child, desperate not to encounter yet another reminder of how much they don't matter. We need to be morally highly evolved to guess at the pain that runs beneath the bluster. People who are most severely ill don't always make the most charming patients; help is the thing they most desperately crave and yet are extraordinarily adept at making sure they won't receive.

When we can manage it, we should disregard the surface antics of the grandiose. We should behave like loving parents who know that their child's angry tantrums spring from fear rather than evil and that their assertions that they hate us are only disguised pleas for relief from the pain of needing us so much.

It is a sign
of immense
psychological
privilege to
know how to be
ordinary.

We will have learnt to be truly kind when we can more reliably keep in mind the angry, lost, tearful, neglected, vulnerable small person who dwells beneath the unpleasant rantings of the blustering, over-confident adult.

Criticism

To be criticised is never pleasant. It is rarely a good day when we have to read an unflattering post about ourselves, when we are given tart feedback on a project or hear that we are being gossiped about or denigrated by strangers or colleagues.

However, the question of how much criticism needs to hurt depends on an aspect of individual psychology that is independent of the specific attack we happen to face. The degree to which we buckle in the wake of negative comments, the scale of the pain that is unleashed by an unflattering remark or mean-minded attack is a function of how we feel about ourselves. When we carry within us a sufficient ballast of love, criticism need never be much more than niggling. We can overcome it by dinner time – or at least by the end of the week. We can take on board with relative good humour that we are not loved by everyone, that not everything we do is perfect and that there may be one or two outright enemies who would prefer us dead, even while most people tolerate us easily enough. There need be nothing surprising or terrifying in being doubted by a few others.

But for the more vulnerable ones among us, there is no option but to experience criticism as an assault on our right to exist. We don't hear that we are being mildly upbraided for an aspect of our work; we feel that we are being told to disappear. It isn't just one or two people who are mocking us, the whole world is thinking only of how ridiculous we are. We will never get past this moment of negative assessment; the hatred will never end.

If criticism from outside proves devastating, it is because it so readily joins forces with an infinitely more strident and more aggressive form of criticism that has long existed inside of us. We are already struggling so hard to tolerate ourselves against inner voices that assert how undeserving, ugly and devious we are, to the extent that there is no room left for us to take on further reminders of our sinful natures. The key of present criticism has inserted itself into a lock of historic hatred and let loose an unmasterable surge of self-loathing.

To lessen the burden on ourselves, we should remember that we aren't exceptionally weak in the face of criticism; we probably had a far worse childhood than the average. Once upon a time, we were almost certainly humiliated and shamed without being soothed or reassured, and this is why we now take current criticism so much to heart. We don't know how to defend ourselves against our enemies because we have never been able to build up ready answers as to why we might be acceptable and good. We already hate ourselves so much more than our worst enemies ever will. A part of us is responding to adult challenges with the vulnerability of a child who faced disdain on a scale they couldn't master. The present challenge feels like a catastrophe because catastrophe is precisely what was once endured.

We may not easily be able to stop feeling unhappy about criticism, but at least we can reorient what we feel unhappy *about*. It need not be a sign that we are actively awful, it is evidence that we were long ago denied the love we needed to remain faithfully and generously on our own side.

Suicide

It is natural to assume that people end up taking their own lives when something of unparalleled awfulness befalls them: they make a grievous error in their work, they mess up a relationship, they flout one of their society's taboos, they are exiled and disgraced.

But the reality is that there are no mistakes or problems that have to lead people to their deaths. There are entrepreneurs who have gone bankrupt and immediately shot themselves, and others who have blithely shrugged off their misfortunes and gone on to live another half century without too much regret. There are people who have been written about in hostile terms in newspapers and been able to dismiss the attacks as irrelevant, and others who have seen no option but to do away with themselves after the first mocking articles have run.

If self-love deserves such sustained attention as a topic, it is because its shortfall is what can, in acute cases, be responsible for a choice to end one's own life. People don't kill themselves because bad things happen to them, they kill themselves because they are already suffering from intense self-hatred, which an unfortunate event or two serves to corroborate and then expand into an unanswerable argument for self-extinction.

No human who has ever been heartily and reliably loved for years by another kindly one will easily take their own life. They will be too often reminded that they once mattered immeasurably and may therefore once again prove of value, so long as they are given the chance to make amends and recover their poise. The baby who is held, kindly tickled, sympathised with and gently soothed isn't just being indulged in the present, they are being given a life-long immunity from the temptation to do away with themselves when hostile winds start to blow.

If we are visited by the urge to kill ourselves, one of the many reasons why we should pause is that we are misdirecting our anger. We aren't the ones who deserve to be killed (or at least blamed), it's the people who at the outset would have needed to make us feel supremely valued and didn't. We aren't perfect, but nor should we have ever expected that we needed to be in order to continue to have claims on existence. Confronted by disasters, we should forgive ourselves in the way we should once have been forgiven; we should be kind towards our battered and destroyed name in imitation of the love that was our due at the outset. There is no need, ever, to kill ourselves; there is only a need to recover contact with the love that should have been our universal birth right.

IV
The Origins of
Self-Hatred

How unloving parents raise self-hating children

A central fact about early childhood is that babies are born into the world entirely at the mercy of others. They have no native strength, intelligence or utility; they cannot fight or complain, walk away or argue their case; their survival depends solely on their capacity to look up from their cots with vast innocent beautiful eyes and charm their parents into caring for them. It's their power to attract love that ensures they will be fed and clothed, protected and kept alive.

In exchange for this nurture, young children readily offer their parents or caregivers unconditional admiration. They naturally adore and are boundlessly impressed by those who pick them up and bathe them, warm their milk and change their sheets. They are in awe at these giant people who know how to turn on a washing machine and kick a ball over a tree. At this stage, there is no innate desire to question or doubt figures of authority.

Given what is at stake, it follows that small children are instinctively sensitive to how well they are doing at getting their admired protectors on their side. If they feel they are loved, they can relax into themselves and get on with the many other pressing priorities of early childhood: working out how to open a drawer, figuring out what a plug socket is, what words are and how life might be enjoyed.

But if love is in more restricted supply, the picture grows more complicated. There are childhoods in which, for a variety of reasons, parents fail to be as charmed as they might be. They leave the baby to scream, they shout at one another, there might be violence and hysteria, lethargic despair and terror. The young child knows instinctively it is in grave danger; if the situation is not somehow corrected, in extremis, it may be left on a hillside to die.

At this point, our biology initiates a desperate yet darkly logical process. The young child starts to try a lot harder. It redoubles its efforts to charm, to be good, to do what could be expected of it, to smile and to ingratiate itself. It wonders what may be wrong with itself to explain the parental disapproval and harm, and doesn't feel any alternative but to search in its own character and behaviour for answers.

At the same time, the child resists what might from one

perspective seem like the obvious move: to get annoyed with and blame the adults in the vicinity who are not looking after it as they should. Such a bold thought does not belong to the defencelessness of the early years. We are in no position to mount a challenge to our protectors when we can hardly reach the door handle, let alone turn on a tap; we need to have our own front door key and bank account before cynicism is a realistic option. It is far more intuitive to wonder why we are horrid than to complain of being treated unfairly and unkindly.

Small children naturally turn injury done to them into dislike of themselves. They ask not so much 'Why does my parent fail to care for me?' as 'How might I have failed this admirable person?' They hate themselves rather than doubting those who should be protecting them; shame replaces anger. It feels, on balance, like the safer option.

A vicious spiral of self-hatred then sets in. The unloved growing child wonders constantly about their faults. Their parent may be an alcoholic, narcissistic, sadistic or depressed; they may never cook a proper meal or they may shout intemperately from their bedroom, but none of that matters. The parent cannot be envisaged as anything other than impressive. To explain the lack of love from the paragons of parenthood, it must be that the child is an awful person, they must be stupid and mean, selfish and slow, physically repulsive, irritating and shallow.

As childhood gets left behind, much of this dynamic is forgotten. The adolescent and young adult overlooks exactly what went on. They cannot think clearly of the early years – and parental figures may be keen that they never do so. Instead of an honest psychological exploration, there is the sentimentality of the photo album and the evocation of the more cheerful moments of family holidays. The former child can't tell any more that their feeling of shame has specific origins; it can feel like something they might have been born with, or a natural phenomenon like bad weather or the flu.

Liberation awaits us when we take on board a highly implausible idea: that our self-hatred, far from being inevitable, is an internalisation of early deprivation and that far from needing to revere and admire those who denied us love, we are in a position to understand, to question, to be annoyed and to mourn what we did not receive. We are not so despicable after all; we've just lacked any better ideas to explain why we didn't manage to charm those who should have been on our side from the start.

66

Emotional neglect

When we imagine the difficulties involved in a so-called bad childhood, we most readily think in terms of children who are physically harmed – beaten, underfed, sexually abused – or else treated with active contempt: screamed at, blamed, put down, mocked and tormented.

Such harrowing images make it hard for us to picture that there might be another form of injury to which children can be exposed, in many ways more prevalent and just as damaging. In this case, there is no physical violence, no taunting or shouting. At first glance it looks as if all must be well. But that would be to miss the particular kind of wound that can be inflicted through what psychologists term 'emotional neglect'.

We're so used to focusing on abuse that springs from interventions, we can forget the abuse that flows from absence. The emotionally neglected child isn't screamed at or hit, locked up or jeered at. They are just *ignored*, often very subtly. A parent doesn't smile at them very much. There is never any time to take a look at the drawing they just did or the story they wrote. No one remembers their stuffed animal's name. No one notices that they are looking sad and that the first day at school might have been difficult. There's always something more urgent to do than spend time with them (perhaps another sibling to think about or the demands of work or of their partner; there might be a lot of parties as well). The parent seems in no way charmed or interested. There are no cuddles or hair ruffles, there are no nicknames or terms of endearment. Birthdays get forgotten. Tears aren't dried or consoled. The parent doesn't look the child in the eye.

At first glance, none of this may seem especially bad, particularly because the insidious behaviour is largely invisible. It is compatible with all kinds of outward signs of healthy family life. There can be emotional neglect in a beautiful home with a large and well-stocked fridge and a swimming pool in the garden. Emotionally neglected children may be sent to the best schools and equipped with tutors and nannies. Everything can look very sane and privileged.

But that isn't to say that severe damage isn't being done. The 19th-century psychologist William James observed that it might be as bad, if not worse, to be on the receiving end of indifference as of physical torment: 'No more fiendish punishment could be devised, were such a thing possible, than that one should be turned loose in society and remain absolutely unnoticed by all the members thereof. If no one turned around when we entered, answered when we spoke, or minded what we did, but if every person we met "cut us dead", and acted as if we were non-existent things, a kind of rage and impotent despair would before long well up in us, from which the cruellest bodily torture would be a relief'.

Rage and impotent despair are precisely what a child may feel when they register the extent to which they don't matter to those who brought them onto the earth, even if these people have never punched them in the back of the head or stopped them having an allowance, except that the rage and despair are unlikely to be conscious and cleanly felt. It is far more likely that these emotions will mutate into a feeling of shame, comingled with continued admiration and respect for those who elicited it.

A categorical fact of psychological life is the disinclination of any child to think that there is something wrong with its parent, even when there very much is; it will go to almost any lengths to prevent the idea emerging that its parent may be mentally unwell or fundamentally brutish. It will remain attached to and obsessed with the most vicious and uncaring figure whom an objective observer would see through in an instant.

The child will do anything rather than think that an injury has been done to it by its progenitor – especially if the parent is charming to other people and impressive in the professional sphere. The child will just assume that there must be something deeply wrong with itself to justify the indifference. It must have failed in some way; it must in its essence be profoundly ugly, repulsive or lacking. This is the only conceivable explanation for the blankness with which its existence is received.

The adult who emerges from such a complicated, veiled childhood is likely to be in a confused state. On the surface, they may experience only a continued desire to please their early caregivers. But deep within themselves, they may feel lacerating doubt, paranoia and self-contempt. To numb such feelings, they may take to drink or develop numbing, calming addictions to keep themselves from encountering their perceived repulsiveness.

A measure of resolution comes when we can take on board the term 'emotional neglect' and treat it, and thereby our own stories, with requisite seriousness. Our childhood sorrows may not rank among the most obvious or newsworthy, but they may be substantial and genuine nevertheless. Our levels of shame attest as much. We were not hit, but we were injured. We failed to receive the love that makes people firm and whole, that allows them to feel authentic and deserving, that prevents them from being impressed by those who mistreat them and that stops them wanting to kill themselves when they mess up.

How we should have been loved

We hear so much about how difficult childhoods can damage people that we sometimes fail to consider the fascinating and telling obverse: What happens in emotionally nurturing families? What does it mean to be properly loved and looked after, and how do people turn out differently when they have been?

In the course of a childhood that can count as properly loving, we might expect some of the following to unfold:

In the early days and months, a beloved young child is placed at the very centre of the parental universe. For a time, they are the one around whom everything else revolves. When they scream for milk, others come quickly; when they pull their first smile, others are amazed; if they have something to say, others listen. Such focus is not a recipe for limitless egoism; we can only hope to become properly modest and able to take care of others when we have had an early taste of total omnipotence. A fulsome experience of infantile egoism is what underpins the selflessness of the future adult.

In a loving childhood, the offspring can expect to be granted a sense that it truly pleases its own parents – not by anything it does, but by its sheer existence. It experiences the full force of primal parental delight, with its arrival being a much anticipated and fulsomely positive act in the parents' lives. This impression is built up from the most minor, everyday moments: the parents light up when it comes into the room, there are warm kisses in the morning and the evening, its pictures are pinned to the fridge, its concerns are registered and its joys remembered.

From this, the child acquires a basic trust in itself and in its right to be. It won't feel meek and cowed. It won't have to apologise for its appetites or hold back on expressing its wishes. It won't get stuck with sadistic or inconsiderate people; it will know how to exit bad relationships quickly. Without any sense of entitlement, it will believe it has a place in the world – and if things ever go seriously wrong, it will know how to take its own side against fate with necessary compassion and tolerance.

In a loving childhood, an offspring benefits from sympathetic interpretations of its behaviour and motives. If it spills something in the kitchen, it isn't a 'clumsy idiot', it's just easy to spill things from those new sorts of cartons. When it doesn't want to share its toys with another child, it isn't a 'selfish rascal', it is expressing a legitimate attachment to its property, no different from what an adult would experience if it had to give up their car or spouse to a random stranger. The loving parent knows not to make the child the villain of the mishaps that come its way.

A loving parent knows that a certain amount of awkward behaviour belongs to every life and they don't shame the child for slipping up or for being sometimes in a tricky temper and fed up with everything for a while. The parent has the confidence to know that sunnier seasons will return and that the child cannot feel real unless it has been given plenty of opportunities to display its full rage and disappointment with the state of things, including school, its siblings, the end of films, bedtimes – and the many faults of its own sometimes profoundly annoying parents.

A loving parent gives the child the sense that it is capable of interesting discoveries and ideas of its own. Rather than rush to the park as though there were an immovable appointment with the swings or the climbing frame, the parent allows themselves to be taken off course by the child's curiosity. Perhaps there is a mesmerising brick wall that needs to be investigated and stroked, with its variety of ever so slightly different bricks, some of which are very smooth to the touch, others far rougher – and one or two of which harbour little tufts of miraculously soft moss. Maybe there is an extremely beautiful small flower growing by a wall that calls for a song to be sung in its honour.

There might be a puddle that is asking to be crossed and splashed through or for small leaves to be scattered across its intriguing silvery surface. There may be a snail dragging itself out on the pavement that throws the whole afternoon in a new direction, because this creature needs to be thoroughly discussed, researched and perhaps even brought home to the garden on a leaf. Charles Darwin or Alexander von Humboldt surely never stumbled upon anything more exciting in their far-flung journeys of exploration.

In a loving childhood, the offspring isn't incited to admire its parent or caregiver more than would be good for its own confidence. The grown-up may have a few strengths, but the child is gently inducted to know that they are only human, with everything this bathetic term entails. Sometimes they are silly, occasionally they are lazy, they can be greedy for chocolate after supper and addicted to daft TV programmes. Through close-up acquaintance with such flaws, a child can in time outgrow the adult and feel able to take their place alongside them in the grown-up realm. The child can in addition come to terms with their own frailties, for if the adult whom they most revere is far from consummate, then their own imperfections can also be faced up to and accepted without shame. One can slip up, be an idiot and still prove worthy enough.

If these emotional ingredients are transmitted in the course of an upbringing, then their recipient can in their adult future be counted upon to know how to be straightforward about their needs, sympathetic to their

The loving parent knows not to make the child the villain of the mishaps that come its way.

errors, ready to escape the clutches of unkind people, able to love others and, most crucially, free to direct compassion towards themselves for their own less than perfect but always still adequate lives.

Reasons for poor parenting

Given how important it is to be properly loved by one's parents in order to have an emotionally sane grown-up life, one may wonder why, in cases that range from the regrettable to the truly tragic, the process can go so wrong. Why do some parents, who might in other areas be decent and thoughtful characters, fail so badly at being able to love the small people they have brought into the world?

Among the many possibilities, two stand out in particular. The first stems from one of the most obvious and unavoidable features of early childhood: an infant arrives on earth in an entirely and almost shockingly vulnerable state. It cannot move its own head, it is utterly reliant on others, it has no understanding of any of its organs, it is in a penumbra of chaos and mystery, it cannot regulate itself or any of its functions. In such helpless circumstances, it must look up to others and beseech them for their mercy: it must ask them to bring it nourishment, to stroke its head, to bathe its limbs, to comfort it after a feed, to make sense of its fury and sadness.

This primal helplessness takes a very long time to dissipate. Even after two or three long years, the offspring is still weak, confused, incompetent and fragile. Its fingers are no thicker than twigs, it could be killed by a family dog, its mind is filled with a plethora of dazzlingly peculiar, unrealistic and sentimental notions. It thinks that teddy bears are alive, it has conversations with plants, it looks forward to Santa coming down the chimney, it wants to stand in circles holding hands with other diminutive people and sing songs about fairies and mummies and daddies, and later draw pictures of giant flowers and friendly butterflies before falling asleep sucking its thumb and nursing its comfort blanket.

To most people, all this is just sweet. But in order to take care of a very small person, an adult is forced to undertake a very particular kind of emotional manoeuvre, one that happens so intuitively and speedily in most of us, we tend not to notice it unfolding: we are required to access our own memories of ourselves at whatever age our young and tender child happens to be, so that we can more precisely deliver to it the care and attention it needs.

It looks from the outside as if we are simply getting down on our knees to play princesses with a child, answering its call for a tasty meal, patiently buttoning up its cardigan to protect it from the cold and adjusting its small woollen hat for the trip to the shops. But in order to make such moves, a part of us has to dig back into our past and imagine ourselves in the role of the small person we are caring for, drawing on our very private reminiscences of ourselves and our bodies in order to sympathise with the sorrows, share in the joys, ameliorate the clumsiness and tend to the urgent crying.

Though at times childcare may be exhausting, most adults have no problem connecting with the child version of ourselves. But this ability is far from natural or spontaneous: it is a function of health and a consequence of a degree of emotional privilege. For a more disadvantaged sort of parent, however, the task of care-via-identification is too challenging. Somewhere in them, a wall has been built, many metres thick and topped with razor wire, between their adult and their child selves. Something in their childhoods was so difficult, they do not and cannot return there imaginatively. Perhaps there was a parent who died, or who touched them in a way they shouldn't or who left them bereft and humiliated. Things in their childhoods were uncomfortable to such an extent that their whole adult identities have been founded on a thorough refusal to re-encounter the helplessness and vulnerability of their early years. Never, not even for twenty minutes while dinner is in the oven, will they get on the floor and remember the child they once were in order to play with the child in front of them.

This kind of adult may have become extremely competent in the professional world. Their manner is likely to be decisive and strong, their opinions robust and their character drawn towards irony, cynicism and a stoic (or plainly tough) approach to trouble, their own and that of others. They may like to say that they have 'no regrets' and that there is 'no use crying'. In theory, they have nothing against looking after a child – they want to be a parent and might have fought hard to be one in the first place – it is simply that they don't realise that they cannot parent properly unless and until they have come to terms with the child version of themselves.

So long as their own vulnerability appals them, they will

secretly and unconsciously be opposed to and untouched by the vulnerability of their own child. They won't be able to be patient with the little person's clumsiness and confusion; they will have no interest in playing with teddies; they will think it pathetic how tearful their child has become because a four-leaf clover got crumpled or a favourite book has a tear in it. Despite themselves, they may end up saying, 'Don't be so silly' or even 'Stop being so childish' when the child cries that one of the toy elephant's eyes is broken; they may brusquely bathe the child and refuse to read it the bedtime story that it is calling for.

There can follow a second characteristic and associated failing in a parent: unresolved envy. However peculiar it can sound, a parent may envy their own child for the possibility that it might have a better childhood than they had, and will unconsciously ensure it won't. Though ostensibly committed to the care of the child, the parent will struggle against an impulse to inflict against it some of the very same obstacles they faced: the same neglect, the same uncaring school, the same lack of help with their development ... A new generation will have to suffer afresh.

In order to parent properly, not only do we need to connect with our memories of our own childhoods, we need to be able to come to terms with our deprivations so as not to feel jealous of those who might have a chance not to endure comparable ones in turn. But a certain kind of traumatised parent remains at some level a needy, disappointed child who would find it unbearable that another child had more than they did. They are like a tormented and tormenting sibling in a disadvantaged household who takes out their pain on someone more helpless, scrupulously making sure that the other child is as sad and lacking as they are.

We cannot help having had the childhoods we had. But if we are planning to have a child, we have a responsibility to ensure that we have a sane relationship to our own pasts: able to access them for reserves of tenderness and empathy, and able not to feel envious of those who do not have to partake in their sufferings. We will be properly grown up when we are in a position to give our offspring the childhood we ourselves deserved, not the childhood we had.

Politics

Many of the reasons why we may hate ourselves come down to psychological and intimate factors, bound up with dynamics in our families and events in our childhoods. But certain other reasons deserve to be thought of as more closely connected up with what one might term the larger forces of history, with the religious, economic and cultural canvas against which we find ourselves. To put it at its most acute, there may be *political* reasons behind our self-hatred.

Some of our difficulty, paradoxical though it can sound, stems from the modern world's insistence on the generous idea that each of us has unlimited potential. The democratic, egalitarian temper of the modern age has fallen on the side of optimism about the human animal and its chances of self-realisation. Gone are the old beliefs about original sin, about inherent mediocrity, about the need to know one's place and not press above one's station. In place of such self-limiting philosophies have come concepts of self-development and growth, of fulfilling one's destiny and living up to one's full scope and talent. Each of us should be able to make an enormous amount of our lives, so we are told; we could rise to the highest peaks of professional fulfilment, make fortunes, be known to and admired by millions; the only thing holding us back is our own imagination.

This sounds extremely kind, and in a sense it may be. But it contributes to a punitive and coercive ideology. For most of human history, our potential may have been limited by strictures of class and education, but we were at least spared the notion that we had failed in relation to an ideal of huge success and prosperity. Our mediocrity, though harsh, was to be expected and interpreted as a general rule rather than an individual lapse. It was not our fault that we were of modest means, obscure, professionally frustrated, unhappily married, less than perfect-looking and in poor health. This was simply the unremarkable norm.

We have not been afforded the luxury of such pessimism. Any failing or difficulty now has to be interpreted as potentially removable; therefore, its stubborn persistence has to be viewed as stemming from a personal deficiency. Not only are we unhappy and forgotten, the explanation for being so lies with us: with some defect in our own characters, with some weakness in our own wills. In the meantime, the mass media does not let up showing us examples of people who have overcome adverse circumstances: this neglected child who became a tycoon, that under-confident introvert who founded a tech empire. If they can do it, then we all can. However, the sterner afterthought is: Why, in that case, are we still languishing? Why are we still living as we are? Why have we failed so conclusively?

There is nowhere left to hide. In England in the medieval period, the poor were popularly known as 'unfortunates', quite literally, pitiful souls who had not been blessed by the gods of fortune. They were to be subjects of charity, not objects of condemnation or moralism. Their destitution was not willed or self-created; it was a tragic and forgivable accident of fate. The modern world has left us no such handy explanations. Those at the bottom of society, especially in the United States, the nation that has done more than any other both to proclaim our opportunities and at the same time to damn our failures, are known simply as 'losers', people who have fairly lost in a meritocratic and unrigged system of preferment, an unimpeachable race of life in which the laggards have only themselves to blame for their lowly placements.

It is no wonder that, in the circumstances of modernity,

failure has grown psychologically far harder to endure than ever before, even as the material consequences of a modest life are, in many places, less severe than they have ever been. The burden is to our self-esteem and sense of ourselves. It may be impossible for us to harbour any respect for who we are, given how little we have managed to make of our apparently infinite possibilities. In relation to the paragons we should have been, how little we can esteem our reality: our fractious relationships, our bitter jobs, our lowly friends ...

We can't blame divine forces or even the workings of a corrupt ruling elite. We are forced to conclude that responsibility lies solely with us, with our miserable levels of intelligence, our unrealistic dreams and sordid and fledgling capacities. It is darkly logical that rates of suicide in advanced economies should be so much higher than those in more modest, god-fearing, resigned societies: Who else could there be to blame for one's disasters but oneself?

It can be hard to imagine that some of the causes of our distemper might lie in the political arrangements of society. To suffer from self-hatred is to be convinced that we and we alone must be held accountable for our failings.

But our readiness to personalise our disapproval is a symptom of our illness rather than a reflection of reality. We may have slipped up here and there and are inevitably foolish and flawed in key aspects. However, our recovery will depend on our willingness to entertain the idea that we did not come to loathe ourselves by nature, that we are the products of families and societies, history and politics that have importantly helped the dark process along, and that we will arrive at greater tolerance and sympathy for who we are when we can at last have enough self-belief to imagine that it was not, in the end, all our fault.

V

The Art of
Self-Acceptance

Becoming historians of ourselves

Few of us who suffer from self-hatred are cleanly aware that we do so. We know the symptoms – the self-doubt, the paranoia, the impostor syndrome, the emotional masochism – but it is counter-intuitive and arduous to trace these troubles back to a singular illness that can be unpicked and assuaged. It may take a good while, perhaps half a lifetime, before we are able to name what has been destroying us all along.

There is a temptation to treat our difficulties narrowly as phenomena of the here and now; we focus on our fears of disappointing our current colleagues, we are revolted by how we look today, we feel in danger of imminent attack and judgement. It takes a bold leap of the mind to imagine that our current feelings about ourselves could derive from our own histories.

Our sense of ourselves, rigidly contemporary though it proposes itself to be, is almost always the residue of how others in the distant past made us feel. We like or dislike ourselves to the extent that we were once liked or disliked by those in whose orbit we developed. It is merely another regrettable symptom of our disease that we find it so hard to keep our own past in mind and have difficulty using it to correct and nuance how we view our present challenges.

A priority of treatment is therefore to become better historians of our own emotions. We stand to discover that we don't just hate ourselves per se, we developed into people who instinctively do so because of the cumulative impact of a number of scenes, characters and atmospheres. These should be retrieved from memory with the patience and deftness of a historian, rooting back in the archives to reassemble the reality of a long-forgotten monarchy or revolution.

Long before there was the current feeling of unease, there would have been someone whose voice we internalised. They might have shamed us about our appearance, or given us a feeling that we were a grave disappointment to them or that we could never measure up to a favoured sibling. They might have ignored us for long stretches, or hit us, or worse. We might have had to observe their rages or tended to them through their depression or manipulative bitterness at an age when we were barely able to look after ourselves.

These incidents led us unconsciously to draw vague yet powerful conclusions about our characters: that there must be something dark and awful about us, that we will invariably be a nuisance to others, that we are selfish and corrupted, that we are the inferiors of those who harm us, that we must appease bullies. We will have forgotten that we came to such conclusions or the reasons why we did so, but that we feel about ourselves as we do today is testament to the historical legacies we are carrying.

As part of our historicising efforts, we might prompt ourselves to finish certain sentences: *My mother made me feel … My father gave me the sense that … Compared to my sibling, I believed I was …* From such blunt instruments, we can assemble a rough first draft of the verdicts that were surreptitiously handed down to us. But we should then move beyond the headlines to remember some of the precise sensory memories that underpin them. When we think of being made to feel ashamed of ourselves, we can wonder what scenes come to mind from the early years.

We should close our eyes and dwell on what spontaneously emerges when we reflect on our beginnings. We should attend to our impressions with the care of a novelist, drawing our fragile intuitions from the penumbra of time to let them resonate, with all their painful echoes, in the here and now. What kind of day was it? Where were we? How old were we? What did we apparently do wrong? What were we crying about? Can we remember how it ended? What must it have been like that night for us?

With the right sort of prompts and sufficient time on our hands (maybe a quiet hour in bed), we can be reminded of how much denser our past is than it seems day-to-day. There is so much that happened to the smaller version of us, and that is still there in our mental archives, waiting for us to be able to muster the courage and compassion to take a look. Through meditating on ourselves, we may newly remember being 5 or so and overhearing a conversation between our mother and our aunt about how unfortunate-looking we were, and how much this seared us and made us cry and fed a feeling that we could never be good enough. Perhaps we were 7 and on the running track and came fifth in an important race and remember the anger on our father's face and a feeling that we would never be able to satisfy this heroic figure even though we desperately wished to make him proud of us.

We learnt the language of self-hatred over many long years. To unlearn it will be a comparably lengthy process.

We will need to go back and make sense of dozens of scenes of humiliation and unloveability. We will need to re-experience a pain that, at another level, we are profoundly committed to running away from, even as it infects our every contemporary hope for ourselves. For a time, we will need to be angry as we have never been before about scenes that reveal themselves, to objective adult eyes, to be inherently unfair and regrettable. Would we have treated a 5-year-old in that way? Is it right for any child to endure such demands? Who might we have been if we had been handled with greater patience? We can see that there is an alternative to the pitiless conclusions we originally reached when, as children, we concluded that the fault lay entirely with us.

We may have to cry in a way we never have before about sorrows and let-downs we plainly didn't merit. There might be long periods when we feel plunged into a new and unfamiliar despair at everything we have been through. It might seem as if we are hitting a fresh low, but with any luck, this will be part of a necessary catharsis, a step towards reaching a condition of greater self-acceptance and inner lightness. We are not inherently awful, we may eventually conclude, we just had a difficult start in life that we are at last on the way to understanding and contextualising.

Anger

We know so much about the dangers of unacceptable anger – of rage, physical harm, petulance and entitlement. Our societies leave us in no doubt as to the risks of getting cross with other people. But this well-meaning drive towards peaceability threatens to bring about another sort of harm, the kind that follows when legitimate grievance is throttled, and justifiable anger is too quickly swallowed. We can be damaged as much when anger is denied as when it is disproportionately expressed.

We, the self-hating ones, may not even have noticed how hard it is for us to tell someone that they have treated us harshly. We are inclined by our pasts always to excuse those who infringe on our interests and needs and give way to self-laceration and despair instead. The rare occasions when we build up the courage to speak are likely to be followed by long periods of unfocused guilt.

We typically stay silent because we come from a past in which nothing inspired us to expect that we could speak freely. We may have grown up in an environment in which no one wanted to hear our contrary or 'difficult' opinions. Under the guise of a devotion to 'good manners' or

We can be damaged as much when anger is denied as when it is disproportionately expressed.

'discipline', the adults left no room for feedback. There were only certain people who were able to express themselves at will, who were allowed to raise their voices and be sadistic or unreasonable – and they were not the children.

As a result, our anger, which should have emerged outwards, was retained and turned against us. We have come to hate ourselves in lieu of any opportunity to register hatred towards those who do and have done us an injury.

Emotional healing depends on a curious-sounding exercise: before we can be serene and balanced, indeed in order that we can be so, we will have to get more skilled at being for a time less than forgiving and no longer so patient. We will need to take lessons in getting fruitfully annoyed and in experiencing anger with those who have injured us, even if we do this only in our own minds – the targets of our frustration perhaps being now dead or too psychologically blocked to be able to hear us directly.

We should develop the strength occasionally to tell a partner that we are feeling ignored and used. We should tell a colleague that they have not done their fair share.

We might try to explain to a parent that they cannot rely on our goodwill unless they show some understanding of what they have put us through. It will feel deeply uncomfortable when we first try; we may expect that terrible vengeance will be exacted on us for our openness. But we may also discover that those who are truly worthy of our time will be ready to listen to our hurts. We should afford more regularly to exchange self-hatred for lawful and honourable expressions of annoyance.

Beyond people pleasing

It can take a while to see that we aren't merely polite and well mannered; that we are manically on the side of trying to appease the moods and caprices of others at the cost of our own well-being; that we are inveterate people pleasers.

Children have no practical or psychological alternatives to trying to cosy up to those who reject them. They naturally seek to place the explanation for their poor treatment on themselves. Their excuses for their wayward caregivers may go on without end, inspiring lifelong degrees of tainted creativity: the violence they were on the receiving end of wasn't 'just' violence, they will tell themselves: it came from pain, it was a sign of strength, it was in a way justified by the bad school report. The emotional neglect was never as bad as such a term makes out: it was merely an old-fashioned toughness linked to admirable traits such as independence and resourcefulness.

We may throw ourselves into our work at school and subsequently in our career as a way of trying to secure the attention of parental figures who seem not to care that we exist. We may make exceptional efforts with our school projects, with our end-of-year exams, with our scholarship papers, because we aren't only attempting to be good students; we are beneath the surface struggling to be the sort of children and humans that can receive the blessing of their creators. We may become known among our friends as 'over-achievers', but the truth is a great deal more poignant: we are the 'under-loved ones' who work furiously to try to feel legitimate in our own eyes.

We need to come to a dispiriting but emancipating realisation: those who demand to be impressed by their own offspring are not worthy of impressing; they are ill. It may look as if, with just another effort, we may finally secure the notice we long for, but we would be better off accepting the darker notion that we will never turn around someone who hasn't already seen the point of us. A healthy parent does not require a child to perform in order to lend them their attention; they may be pleased when the child is doing well, they may be proud of them at moments of victory, but they do not make performance the sine qua non of their love. This requirement belongs to psychopathology, not aspiration.

The people pleaser needs to learn an unusual and little-mentioned art: that of giving up on people. Rather than continuing to maintain that there must be something wrong with them to explain the sour mood of their caregiver, they should take on board the unfamiliar idea that they have grown up around someone who was severely unwell. Rather than spend their life wondering what is so wrong with them, they can turn the tables and wonder what might have been so wrong with their progenitors for making such peculiar and inordinate demands on them.

We should stop expecting that we are about to be treated well, like an overeager puppy always looking out for signs that their owner has relented and will take them out to the park after all. We have been the lovelorn dog long enough, we have waited for our biscuits for an eternity, and now need to move away from those who exert a mesmeric hold on us by denying us what should naturally have been offered to us a long time ago.

We don't have to keep searching for an offence we haven't committed. We have done well enough at work; we are sufficiently intelligent and decent looking. We have served far too long an apprenticeship in the school of suffering. It is time to make the remarkable discovery that we can dismiss others as they have dismissed us and concentrate for the remainder of our days on those blessed souls who already know how to freely grant us the kindness and approval we are worthy of.

What love really is

Part of the process of overcoming self-hatred involves learning more about what love really is, so that we can detect its absence in the way we treat ourselves and start to nurture and honour its presence in our hearts.

As self-haters, we typically harbour an unhelpfully Romantic view of love, which proposes that love is the reward given to a person for their strengths: it is what someone can expect to receive when they are beautiful, rich, impressive or popular. According to this philosophy, the most loveable person on earth is simultaneously the most gifted and consummate one.

But there is another, broader, nobler conception that understands love not as a reward for strength but as a sympathy for, and commitment to attending to, weakness. Love is what we spontaneously feel when we see a small baby, helpless before the world, reaching out for our finger, clasping it tight and pulling a frail and grateful smile. Love is what we feel when a friend tells us that they cannot cope anymore, that they have reached the end of their tether and are desperate for reassurance and comfort. Love is what we feel when we see a stranger who longs for food and shelter and detect their humanity in their eyes as we buy them some supper and arrange a bed for them for the night. Love is what we register when our partner, usually composed and competent, breaks down and comes to us with apology and confusion, begging for our help.

However impressed we may be by paragons of beauty and flawless achievement, what we truly stand to love in others are displays of vulnerability. We begin to love, rather than merely admire, someone when they no longer have to be perfect and strong, but can instead show us the struggle that is involved in being them, when they let us in on the pain behind their facade of competence.

We should take inspiration from registering when we are moved to redefine our sense of the love we should show ourselves and seek from others. The people we should put our faith in are those who do not recoil from us in our frightened or hesitant moments, those who don't just want to clap at us and be awed by our triumphs. They are those who can be moved by our crises, who are on hand in the dark hours, who we know will still be around when the rest of the world is jeering at us.

Similarly, the properly self-loving person isn't the one who congratulates themselves when they have pulled off an astonishing feat; it's the one who knows how to speak to themselves in a kind voice when it has all gone wrong, who can remain kind in the face of ill fortune, who doesn't have to berate or criticise themselves without mercy. We should feel proud of having attained a capacity for such love. It isn't weakness or charity; it is an achievement founded on the most dignified understanding of what we must do to accede to our full humanity.

We will have finally learnt to love both ourselves and

others when it is fragility and imperfection that touch us and incite our desire to assist, to understand and to console.

Self-forgiveness

Our refusal to forgive ourselves for our mistakes tends to hang on a strong sense of how much these were, in the end, avoidable. We obsessively go back over our slips and errors and contrast what did happen with what could so easily have been skirted if we had not been so fatuous and so witless. We experience recurring jabs of pain at the disjuncture between the agonising present and its now-vanished alternative: we should never have written that email, we should never have become involved with that person, we should have listened more closely to the advice, we should never have borrowed the money ...

Alongside the pain come questions: Why didn't we have greater foresight? Why couldn't we muster more self-restraint? How could we have been so indiscreet? From this close up, there are no realistic, let alone kind, ways to answer our punitive self-interrogations; as a result, they are likely to go on forever, without let up in agony. We will at best conclude that we messed up because we were greedy, because we were vain, shallow, intemperate and weak-willed; that we have ruined our lives because we are lustful, hare-brained, immature and egocentric.

Our self-hatred will grow ever more intense as we contrast our soiled lives with the impeccable choices of others. The reasonable and good ones, the calm and happy ones, had it right all along: they didn't succumb to temptations, they stayed steady and dutiful, they kept their priorities straight and paid due respect to public opinion. The overall conclusion is that we are simply awful people, who should probably (depending on the severity of the problem we are in) kill ourselves forthwith.

If we are to avoid eternal self-loathing or suicide, we will have to find another approach. We cannot forever explain our mistakes by examining this or that local flaw in our characters. We need to lean on a far more holistic and objective answer. We messed up because we are human, which in this context means that we belong to a species that is compelled by its very nature to steer through life without the knowledge and experience required to ensure goodness and wisdom, kindness and happiness.

We may regret this or that error, but from the right

distance, we are fundamentally steering blind and are therefore doomed to slip up with greater or lesser severity at some point or other. We can't know exactly whom we should marry. We don't have fool-proof knowledge of where our real talents lie, let alone how the economy will perform, and therefore can't determine the sort of career we should optimally invest ourselves in. We may make a reasonable guess at what activities and situations might be dangerous, but we cannot know ahead of time exactly where the true risks lie; there are landmines buried everywhere. Assumptions made in one era may fail to be correct in another. We can be caught out by swift changes in mores: what could have been acceptable at one point can turn into an indecency a few years later.

Certainly, we may have experienced a particularly jagged edge of life that has destroyed us in a very specific way. But though the wound is local, the injury is almost endemic. It could have been foretold from the start that something bad would happen to us at some moment, not because there is anything especially deficient about us, but because human brains are lacking the necessary matter to lead us faultlessly through the decades-long obstacle course of life.

That said, our self-contempt tends to be heightened because we refuse to think about luck. We look at where we have ended up and compare it with the more fortunate places of others and come to only one verdict: we must have been more stupid than they are, our characters must have been more corrupt than theirs. But in the process, we miss out on a critical explanatory factor: whatever our flaws may have been, we may have had to contend with a particularly vicious swerve of fate. There have been people every bit as hasty or unreasonable as us who (for now) have sailed on unmolested. Events have pressed more harshly on the vulnerable parts of our personalities. Anyone who would have been tested as we were would have failed in comparable ways. In assessing our destiny, we should remember to claim a very large role for the forces of foul luck.

At the same time, we do ourselves an injury by comparing ourselves only with those above us, rather than considering our state in the round. In our abject moods, we look enviously at those who are presently riding high while failing to consider the hundreds, even millions, of those who have endured destinies every bit as cruel as our own. The human condition has seldom been a smiling one: we should not compound our difficulties by refusing to consider all those who have wept every bit as much as us and lost even more than us.

Nor should we keep equating ourselves with people who, while they might have some superficial similarities with us in terms of age or educational background, in the end had incomparably different psychological beginnings. They didn't have our parents, they didn't have to go through what we did, they didn't have to master our emotional immaturities. They may seem to be our equals but they in fact belong to a more blessed cohort. We should nurture sympathy for ourselves based on a fine-grained appreciation of the specific burdens we had to take on.

A degree of regret may sometimes be helpful: it can help us to take stock of errors and to avoid the worst of the pitfalls next time. But runaway self-hatred serves no useful purpose; it is, in its masochistic way, an indulgence we can't afford. We may be foolish, but this doesn't single us out as particularly awful or unusual; it only confirms that we belong to the human race, a fact for which we deserve limitless sympathy and compassion.

We may be foolish, but this doesn't single us out as particularly awful or unusual.

A loveable idiot

To conclude, after many mistakes and regrets, that we are perhaps at heart idiotic and that is why we have failed is an idea we're inclined to approach in a mood of some bitterness and bile. Our idiocy is hardly something we can be expected to approve of, let alone greet with a smile.

But that is to overlook the extent to which it remains open to us to interpret our idiocy in another way: not simply as an abhorrent and vile fact about ourselves, but as an essentially loveable, endearing trait we share with humanity in general.

The people who have done the most to help us to feel warmly towards our broken natures have been those applied philosophers we more popularly know as comedians. The central characters of comedy are typically extremely imperfect humans; think, for example, of John Cleese's character Basil Fawlty (*Fawlty Towers*) or of Ricky Gervais's David Brent (*The Office*). If we were to meet Fawlty or Brent, we might respond to their misdeeds and lapses with irritation and short-tempered bemusement. How could we possibly forgive a hotel manager as conceited and hot-tempered as Fawlty or a boss as vain and self-absorbed as Brent? Even worse, if we happened to be these people and went through a 3 a.m. moment of lucidity about our personalities, how could we cope with recognising the scale of our absurdity and selfishness?

But the creators of these comedic figures offer us an alternative to contempt. They do not imply that Fawlty and Brent might be decent and unobjectionable people. We are left in no doubt as to the scale of their flaws. What is rare is how we are invited to perceive these flaws – not as just hate-worthy and abhorrent but as deserving of tolerance and good will.

Certainly Brent and Fawlty are idiots, but they are simultaneously something a great deal more morally elevated: they are *loveable idiots*. They are characters whose warps we can notice but treat with generosity, the way that a parent might interpret the wayward slips of a beloved child. The reason a parent can adopt such a stance is that they have a good sense of how difficult it is for the child to do anything other than get things wrong, even as they struggle hard to impress and show themselves in a good light. These parents don't hold their mistakes against them because they know what they are up against: all the immaturity, impulsiveness, disappointment and rage that belongs to early childhood.

Ricky Gervais as David Brent in *The Office*. A loveable idiot.

In a similar way, the comedic creators prompt us to see that Fawlty and Brent, for all their often disastrous antics, are trying their best against enormous odds. They are decent people dragged into ridiculousness by distortions that, in some form or other, they share with almost everyone (including, of course, us): impatience, a desire for applause, lust, a refusal to listen ...

It looks as if we are being encouraged to laugh at Brent and Fawlty, but we are in reality and more deeply being invited to love them – if by love we mean to notice and feel sympathy for all the efforts that humans make to be good, even when what usually results is absurdity, failure and frustration. Laughter fills the gap between what is and what should be; it is the leading, indeed the only real, alternative to despair and self-contempt.

We may well have done many things wrong; we have perhaps let ourselves down and betrayed others' faith in us. But we do not have to despise who we are. We are idiots, yet should strive to belong to the finest variety, the loveable ones, the ones who cannot stop acting in an inept and unbalanced way, but all the while still deserve to be patted, hugged and forgiven.

Original sin

Another way to approach our problematic aspects in a more compassionate way is to conceive of them as symptoms of an inherently and unavoidably 'sinful' side to human nature.

According to the Judeo-Christian story of creation, all humans are fundamentally and radically imperfect. We might once have partaken of godly grace; we carry within us a trace of the divine, but we are also inescapably the heirs of history's gravest sinners. Adam and Eve's transgression did not only taint them, it marked every one of their descendants and ensured that none of us would ever regain the purity that had once been our potential. To listen to the Biblical verdict, we would always be prey to the worst impulses, to greed, destruction, envy, malevolence and fury. That these keep cropping up in our history has been foretold from the start; we have no other options but to err. There could be no sterner reminder of the dangers, and impossibility, of perfection.

Such pessimism may sound cruel and unforgiving, but while it is undoubtedly harsh at a group level, it is highly redemptive and consoling at an individual one. Our errors,

Lucas Cranach the Elder, *Adam and Eve*, 1538. We have by necessity been making a mess of things since the start.

far from being isolated burdens that we alone must carry and proof of an exceptionally wicked aspect of our own characters, are in reality symptoms of an inevitable defect at the core of all our beings. We may have failed and disappointed others in specific ways, but error and mishap have been factored into the human lot since creation.

What might replace fury with ourselves is compassion for *Homo sapiens* as a whole, not just this or that unfortunate member, but the entire damned and wretched assembly. From a religious perspective, this is the moment when we should fall to our knees and beg for mercy: God will offer to love us and redeem us for our brokenness. But even if there is no deity in our worldview, we may still feel a surge of tenderness and fellow feeling when we properly take on board the scale of our collective follies and delusions.

To hate ourselves alone and in private, with intensity and focus, is to miss out on a more bounteous appreciation of our species-wide awfulness, which we should lament rather than castigate ourselves for. There is so much that we might dislike about who we are from close up, but we would be wiser and kinder to step back and feel sorry for the species, which has been making a mess of things since the early fateful days in Eden.

Regression

One of the most striking features of relationships is that, after a while, if things are going well, one or both partners will almost naturally start to refer to the other as 'baby'. They might, alternatively or in addition, stick a diminutive on to the end of their name ('-ie'), buy them a teddy (or show them their own from way back) and late at night speak to them in an unusually high-pitched, soothing and sing-song way.

We all invest a considerable part of our energy and our pride in growing up, in ensuring that we no longer need help in tying our shoelaces, don't need to be reminded to wrap up warm on cold days, and can take care of combing our own hair. In short, we try hard to be adults.

But successful grown-up relationships demand something rather peculiar of us: while we are rewarded for the overall maturity of our characters and way of life, we are also invited, when striving to be close to someone, to access the less developed and more puerile sides of ourselves. It belongs to authentic adulthood to be able in an intimate relationship to curl up like a small child and seek to be 'babied' as one might have been many decades before, when we wore pyjamas with elephant prints on them and had a lisp and a small gap in our front teeth. It belongs to health, rather than pathology, to realise how much one might at difficult moments want to be 'mummied' or 'daddied' by a partner and to connect for a time with the helpless, frightened, dependent child one once was and will at some level always remain.

Sadly though, this selective regression is no easy or charming journey back for those whose childhood involved them in scenes of suffering and humiliation. For them, growing up has required a superhuman effort never again to place themselves at the mercy of those who might take advantage of their vulnerabilities. Returning into imaginative contact with 'mummies' and 'daddies' therefore holds no particular charm; their teddies will not be having a picnic anytime soon.

These bulletproof characters are likely to walk through the world with defiance and strength. They will have built a heavy shield of irony around their hearts. Sarcasm may be their favourite mode of defence – and they will have ensured in a thousand ways that no one would ever attempt to ask them, even in the briefest, most light-hearted and humorous way, to 'come to mummy or daddy' for a hug.

The defensiveness is understandable, but not necessarily aligned with the real requirements of maturity. True health would mean recovering an easy and informal contact with one's less robust dimensions; it would mean being able to play the child because one knew one was resolutely the adult. It would mean being able to be 'baby' because one was in no doubt that one had safely overcome the fears and traumas of the defenceless past.

The more difficult the early years have been, the more of our undeveloped self must be disavowed, the more we must appear grandiose, impregnable and daunting. Nevertheless, we will know we have acceded to genuine adulthood when we can hold out a protective hand to our frail younger selves and reassure them that we will from now on be their reliable guardians and protectors and allow them to visit us for a cuddle and a play whenever they need to.

Habit formation

Change happens not when we hit upon a set of good ideas and assent to their suggestions in passing; it happens when we can turn *theoretical agreement* into something routine, into a *habit*. Most of the valuable lessons we sign up to remain stuck at the level of aspiration because we refuse the rigorous labours we would have to undertake to embed them into the fabric of our lives.

Because we didn't learn to hate ourselves in a day, it will take far more than a moment to move towards a stance of self-acceptance. We should lean on analogies to prepare us for the scale of the task. Our minds are like long-established houses that will need their dividing walls smashed down, their plumbing relaid and new corridors inserted. We have spent decades learning to speak the language of self-loathing and will require hundreds of hours to pick up an alternative dialect of tenderness and generosity. We are a patient with a fractured limb who will have to remaster how to cross a room.

Part of retooling ourselves will mean growing a lot less trusting towards our own minds. Instead of siding with our immediate instincts, we will have to appreciate just how many of these stem from unrepresentative experiences at the hands of corrupted caregivers and will therefore be rife with distortions and omissions. Our minds probably do not give us an adequate understanding of our own relative merits, of the dangers we face or of the true intentions of others. We may wonder far too quickly what we have done wrong when it is in reality the people around us who have hurt us, or we may instinctively be revolted by anyone who chooses to be kind to us. However reliable our minds are in other areas, however logical we may be in certain endeavours, in our emotional reflexes we should allow that we have been mauled by an illness that has crippled our powers of objectivity.

We need to stand back from our impulsive minds and treat them as organs scarred by their pasts, whose certainties we need to examine with the help of all the detached independent intelligence we can muster. We should not too quickly trust who we fall in love with, we should not believe most of our fears, we should not succumb to the voices that assure us we are unworthy; we deserve to fight back against the inner critic who is always on hand to tell us about our disgraceful nature.

Accompanying this suspicion of ourselves should be a wariness around our moods. We should recognise how much we are prey to moods that have a power to transform our view of ourselves and the world without informing us that they have hijacked our minds to nefarious ends. In a mood of exhaustion, we may feel sure that we have conclusively understood who we are: reprehensible beasts whose entire lives have been wasted and who should never have been born – a conclusion that can seem, as we lie in bed in the early hours, as reasonably founded as the seven times table or the theory of evolution.

The problem is that our moods don't do us the favour of announcing themselves as such. They make us trust that whatever we incline to when in their grip is all that we have ever, and will ever, believe. And so, we miss that we hate ourselves not primarily because we are so detestable as because we haven't slept properly in a week, haven't had enough exercise, have been eating heavy foods and are in dire need of conversation with a friend.

As we wean ourselves off our self-hating ways, we should become wary of those situations and routines that can return us to the worst of our inclinations. We should minimise our exposure to media, surround ourselves with enthusiastic and warm-hearted people, avoid pushing ourselves too hard at work and make time to sift through our thoughts at the end of every day. We should embrace a quiet, nourishing lifestyle suitable for the emotional convalescents we are. There is no more need for manic ambition or for striving to be at the centre of things. We should simultaneously note how much our progress can be

123

undermined by contact with envious and hostile articles, by disappointed and vengeful friends, by chaotic busy days and by insincere and greedy colleagues. We are never more than one or two bad habits away from inner collapse.

There is a cacophony of voices inside us. Over the years, it's the destructive, trenchant and sardonic ones that have spoken to us with the greatest authority and been listened to with unending respect. But there are alternatives. We know how to be kind and have been so with others for many years. Now is the moment to extend some of this kindness back to ourselves, to speak as if we were not under any divinely ordained command to mock all we are and to turn every day into a tunnel of fear and distrust.

We won't manage this feat of cordiality very easily. We'll speak in an accent of self-loathing for a good many years yet. But with sufficient care, we stand one day to become more fluent in the language of self-care. When other voices protest that this is not what we deserve, that we must suffer and flail ourselves further, we might decide for once to side with the habits of love, and ignore the sirens of doom, call a friend, switch off social media, put on a Bach cantata, squeeze an orange juice and sit peacefully with our kinder thoughts during a very long, hot bath.

Friendship

One of the most regrettable features of self-hatred is that it denies us a chance to connect properly with other people. So convinced are we of our own awfulness, we hold out no hope that we would ever be able to solicit the sincere attention or tenderness of someone else. We become private, guarded and reclusive out of a suspicion of our warped natures, a certainty that we cannot let another human see who we are for fear of inciting hatred and opprobrium. Insofar as we strive to be sociable, it is through the help of a false self that smiles and ingratiates itself but is careful never to speak with sincerity or spontaneity. We can conceive of no alternative but to keep the world far away from the frightful reality of who we are.

To break out of the cycle of isolation requires a suspension of our normal convictions, a gamble that what is inside us cannot be so very different from what must be in others. There must be a corollary to our fears, vulnerability, doubt, guilt and shame in people in the vicinity; whatever the lack of evidence to the contrary, we cannot have been fashioned in such an exclusively dreadful way.

The gamble requires that we should, without waiting for

the other person to initiate, take a small risk to reveal an aspect of our true and guarded self. We should dare to say that we are feeling out of sorts, that we cannot always cope as we should, that we are beset by fears of disgrace, that we worry that we might be widely hated, that we are prey to envy and inadequacy. We should at last love ourselves enough to tell someone else how much we hate who we are and thereby break out of the closed circle of self-disdain.

Through such a risk, we stand to make a welcome and heart-warming discovery. Such honesty, far from frightening others, is likely to draw them to us and evoke their compassion and loyalty. There will be room for them to assist and reassure us. We will also be doing them an enormous service. Our candour will at a stroke make their own shameful sides less oppressive to them and allow them to unburden in a way they may have longed to do for an age. Our avowals will be a gift to their own lonelier selves.

A friendship will be built up on the best foundations, not around mutual boasting and grandstanding but around shared confessions of regret and weakness. Together we will be able to sympathise with and laugh at the troubles of being human. We will see that difficulty is no bar to

We should at
last love
ourselves enough
to tell someone
else how much
we hate who
we are.

friendship; it is its wellspring. We will realise that we had for years misunderstood what we needed to do to appeal to the world. We thought it was our perfections that would attract admiration; we now see it is our sorrows that cement fellow-feeling.

We should not continue to be the only judges of our lives and deeds. We have shown ourselves to be unfitted to the task: too punitive, extreme and moralistic. We need to divest the responsibility onto a few close friends who can be a constant presence in our lives and – as usefully – in our minds. We can refer to them when we are under siege and benefit from some of their life-giving and merciful perspective. *No, this isn't a reason to kill ourselves. Yes, there would be another way to see this. No, we do have a right to complain.* Through their warm-hearted counsel and tutelage, we can loosen ourselves from the empire of self-hatred we have grown up in and one day become that most precious and life-protective of things: a friend to ourselves.

Breakdown

One of the symptoms of self-hatred is a belief that we must keep going at all costs. We should not let on about how much difficulty we are in, we must never cause anyone the slightest inconvenience (how could they tolerate or forgive us for it?) and we must strive to maintain a permanent front of wholehearted solidity and professionalism.

It sounds admirable, but it is also an unrealistic and unliveable philosophy over the decades. If we are never able to bend, we are at high risk of shattering. Eventually, it may be the greatest help to ourselves (and indirectly to others) if we can allow ourselves to trust that we are not expected to lead entirely perfect lives, if we accept that we can at moments cause a fuss, admit that it is all too much and draw up the white flag – in other words, if we can be flexible enough to have a breakdown.

The word sounds terrifying, especially to the perfectionist residing in the minds of all self-haters. But in reality, a breakdown deserves to be honoured as a stepping stone towards health and replenishment; it may be the tricky but necessary prelude to a breakthrough.

In order to get better, we may have to reach a point where we acknowledge fully how ill we are and therefore have to stop living in the restricted, false, self-abnegating and scared way we have been doing. We may have to hand in our resignation or tell colleagues that we can't be the workhorse they had expected us to be. We may have to admit that we are too frightened and paranoid to continue with our present responsibilities. We may have to tell a partner that we need to separate or renegotiate our union. We might have to lie in bed for a week or a few months and say very little to anyone as we nurse and tend to our exhausted minds.

None of this needs to be fatal. It can be a stage towards greater self-honesty and self-compassion. Self-hatred has held sway over us for too long. It has denied us the chance of good relationships; it has cut us off from other people; it has bred terror and self-contempt; it has hunched our shoulders and pressed down on our bowels. We are owed a moment of rebellion against this unkind and strict regime. We are not hateful people; we have been the unloved ones who are now finally able to see our deprivation for what it is and are in a state of crisis that befits, and can help us overcome, our illness. We will start to get better when we can clearly see how unwell we have been.

VI

Towards a More
Self-Accepting Life

One of the ways in which we can accelerate, and keep faith with, change is to look forward to a time when it has occurred and anticipate what it might be like to have made progress with our psyches. Here is some of what we might expect when we have come to lead more self-accepting lives:

We would not be inordinately pleased with ourselves or bask in an impression of our own wondrousness. We would still be clear-eyed as to our multiple faults; it's just that we would have started to interpret these in a new way. No longer would they be an argument for self-flagellation or for feelings of exceptional wretchedness; no longer would they have to lead to long periods of depression and paranoia. We would be aware both of our shortcomings and of how endemic these are to the race as a whole. We wouldn't feel singled out or persecuted. We would know that we belonged to a sinful and inherently foolish species that had been making a mess of things from the start, and that there were, from a sufficient perspective, few options for us other than to do so in turn.

We would have learnt to cast a benevolent eye on our follies, to treat ourselves like naughty children, deserving of a measure of imagination and sympathy, not monsters

133

intent on causing harm. We would know how rooted our wayward characters were in aspects of our early history and in family dynamics that defied easy understanding and alteration. We would know we were idiots, but, from some angles at least, idiots of the more loveable sort.

We would know that we deserved love not because of how perfect and accomplished we were, but because of how broken and desperate we remained. We would understand that the noblest kind of love springs from sympathy for what is weak and malformed, not from admiration for what is flawless and serene.

We would have learnt how to let other people into our lives and how to bond with them around a shared revelation of fear and dependence. We would let off small signs to others that we understood that they might be going through something similar to us, and that they would be safe with their vulnerabilities in our company. We would have grasped that true friendship demands a sloughing off of pride and an acceptance of our mutual mediocrity and neediness. We would have ensured that our friendships were kindly and humour-filled celebrations of our common eccentricities, disappointments and terrors.

We would be modest about our capacity to love ourselves reliably. We would know that we had for years been struck by a chronic illness and that it could not be overcome in a few weeks or months. We would be committed to managing our symptoms and to carefully shielding ourselves from what might provoke or aggravate our condition. We would be especially careful of media, false friends, overfull diaries and the wrong kinds of professional ambition. But we'd also know that lapses into self-hatred were inevitable and would not castigate ourselves for them too severely when they occurred. There would be no need to hate ourselves for sometimes hating ourselves on top of it all.

Our awareness of how much time we had lost to self-hatred would render us especially sensitive to moments when we were free of the sickness and could engage with our work and with our friends, with nature and with culture without sapping fear and despair. We would be particularly grateful for those days when we could wake up free of dread and could trust that we were deserving and good enough to continue.

With a new assertiveness against self-hatred, we would in addition pick up how to speak to our inner critic in a new and less abject way whenever they visited us in our low moods. Here are some of the answers we might have learnt to give to this ferocious voice:

Inner critic: You're a disgrace.
Self-accepting reply: Of course: I have failed, I have got things wrong, I have been impatient, I have been immature and hare-brained. I know this inside out. But there are limits to how mesmerised one should remain by this appalling insight. I have better things to do than to jump at its mention every time like a soldier to a bugle. I refuse to devote the remainder of my days to a rehearsal of all the particulars of my own unworthiness.

Inner critic: You've made some terrible mistakes.
Self-accepting reply: As we all have. We are all born blind; we stumble in the darkness. We bring our good intentions to bear on the confusing reality of life and give birth to catastrophes. We have been sinners since Adam and Eve. I may be bad, but I am not alone.

Inner critic: You should surely want to die.
Self-accepting reply: That is the easy way out. The challenge is to work out how to continue in the face of all the arguments in favour of taking one's own life. And

there is no better reason than because one is still capable of helping others who, right now, are as lost as we once were.

Inner critic: Look at all those other, amazing people who do better than you.

Self-accepting reply: I have no further interest in comparing my life to theirs. I can't tell what they may be going through inside or what fate could have in store for them. I can only own my own story, with its particular mixture of pain and arduousness. I have done the best I could, within the limited confines of my understanding and with the awkwardness of the cards I was dealt.

Inner critic: You have wasted so much time.

Self-accepting reply: To which the only answer is love: love what remains of our days, love charity, self-forgiveness, mercy, modesty, acceptance, appreciation and gratitude.

Progress will be slow; some days it will seem as though we have learnt nothing at all, but broadly we will be on our way. We will be in recovery from the depredations of self-directed loathing. We will know that we have acquired more fruitful options than to tear ourselves apart. We will have left the shores of self-hatred for the wider, kinder seas of self-acceptance.

Credits

p.113
Ricky Gervais as David Brent in
The Office, 2002. BBC Photo Archive

p.116
Lucas Cranach the Elder, *Adam
and Eve*, 1538. Oil on panel, 59 cm
× 40.5 cm. University of Toronto
Art Centre, Malcove Collection,
Toronto, Canada / Wikimedia
Commons

Self-Knowledge

An examination of the importance of self-knowledge, providing practical exercises to aid self-discovery.

In ancient Greece, when the philosopher Socrates was asked to sum up what all philosophical commandments could be reduced to, he replied: 'Know yourself'. Self-knowledge matters so much because it is only on the basis of an accurate sense of who we are that we can make reliable decisions – particularly around love and work.

This book takes us on a journey into our deepest, most elusive selves and arms us with a set of tools to understand our characters properly. We come away with a newly clarified sense of who we are, what we need to watch out for when making decisions and what our priorities and potential might be.

ISBN: 978-0-9957535-0-1

How to Overcome
Your Childhood

Understand the past, move on to the future

A guide to breaking free from the enduring, and sometimes damaging, behavioural patterns learnt in childhood.

To an extraordinary and humbling extent, who we are as adults is determined by events that happened to us as children. The way we express affection, the sort of people we find appealing, our understanding of success and our approach to work are all shaped by events in childhood.

We don't have to remain prisoners of the past, but in order to liberate ourselves from our histories we must first become fully aware of them. This is a book about such a liberation. We learn that building up an emotionally successful adult life is possible, so long as we reflect with sufficient imagination and compassion on what happened to us a long while back.

ISBN: 978-1-9999179-9-9

The School of Life publishes a range of books on essential topics in psychological and emotional life, including relationships, parenting, friendship, careers and fulfilment. The aim is always to help us to understand ourselves better and thereby to grow calmer, less confused and more purposeful. Discover our full range of titles, including books for children, here:

www.theschooloflife.com/books

The School of Life also offers a comprehensive therapy service, which complements, and draws upon, our published works:

www.theschooloflife.com/therapy